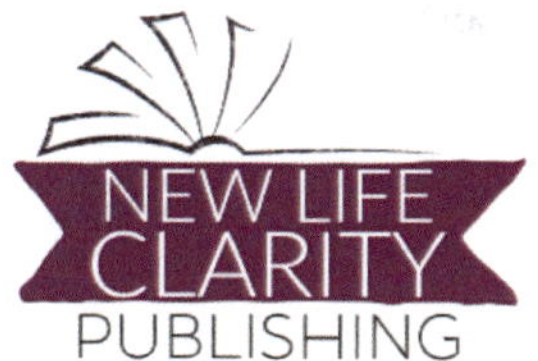

New Life Clarity Publishing

205 West 300 South, Brigham City, Utah 84302

Http://newlifeclarity.com/

Printed in the United States of America
ISBN- 978-1-0879-7883-3
Copyright@2021 G.K.

FROM MY HEART TO YOURS

Poetry & Prose

G.K.

For God
For Mom and Dad
For Alejandra and Santiago
For Abuela and Abuelo
For Alex
For Jason
For Mercedita
For Zoé
For Mr. DeLeon
For the Hernandez Family
For the Sorenson Family
For the Dew Family
For Neruda
For Wilde
For all of my dear readers to
whom I wrote this for

To all that were previously mentioned, I grant you with the most heartfelt thanks that my very soul could bare. My gratitude exceeds beyond verbal expression and I owe you all my most sincere indebtedness. I cannot fathom the tireless patience and guidance that I have received from my publisher, Pattie Sadler. Without you, my voice would not be heard and my heart would be left void of a vessel. Thank you for seeing the potential within me. I would also like to thank Alyssa Naylor for dedicating her time in contributing the beautiful pieces of art that has made this book whole. You are a gift and you have my eternal thanks. To my family, you are the light that has made more room in a heart that was shadowed by doubt and fear. You are my muses and the poetry within me. I would also be delighted in acknowledging the families and friends formally regarded. I am in awe of your support and unconditional love. I am forever devoted in repaying you for all of the gifts that you have given me. I would now like to conclude with thanking my readers. You understand me as I understand you, you see me as I see you, we are all one in the same and I hope to have brought you a home to come back to, a haven to seek refuge in, and a place where you are reminded of your importance. Thank you for your fiery love. You help ignite the furnace within me and thank you for finally showing me how to burn.

The Abyss

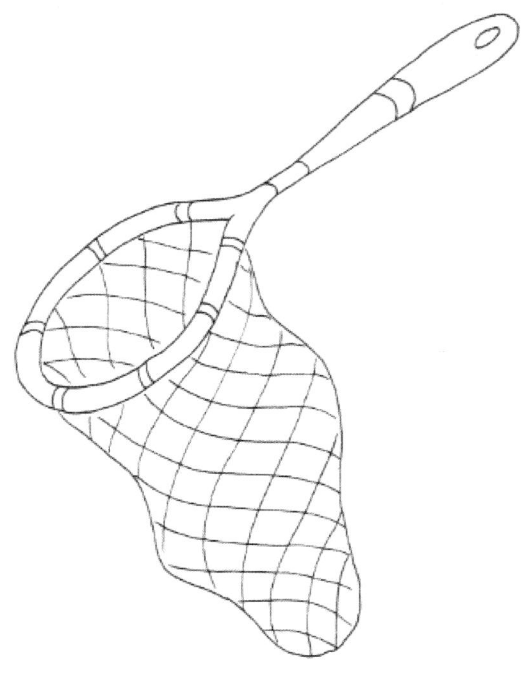

"My Soul's Baggage"

The bags under my eyes
Carry the weight of the nights
Staring at the ceiling
With tears freely falling into no one's palms.
These droplets of pain aren't caught or wiped
As my hands are folded.
Maybe I am my own enemy?

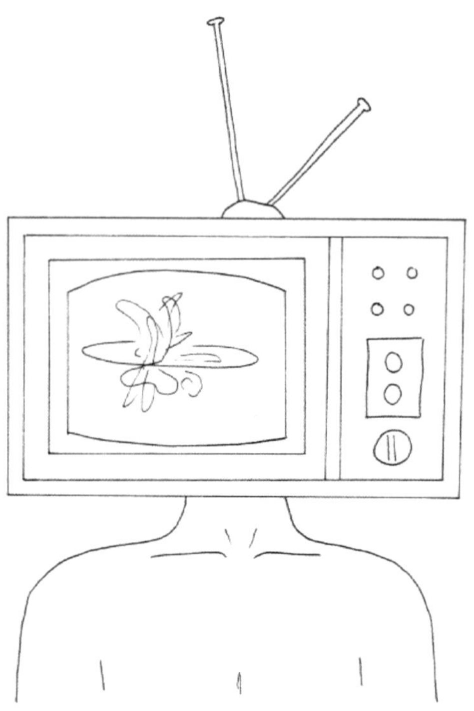

"Cesspool"

These thoughts have made my brain feel like a cesspool.
Memories of joy and memories of anguish
Clash in a dirty mix
In a fight
Over the will of my heart.

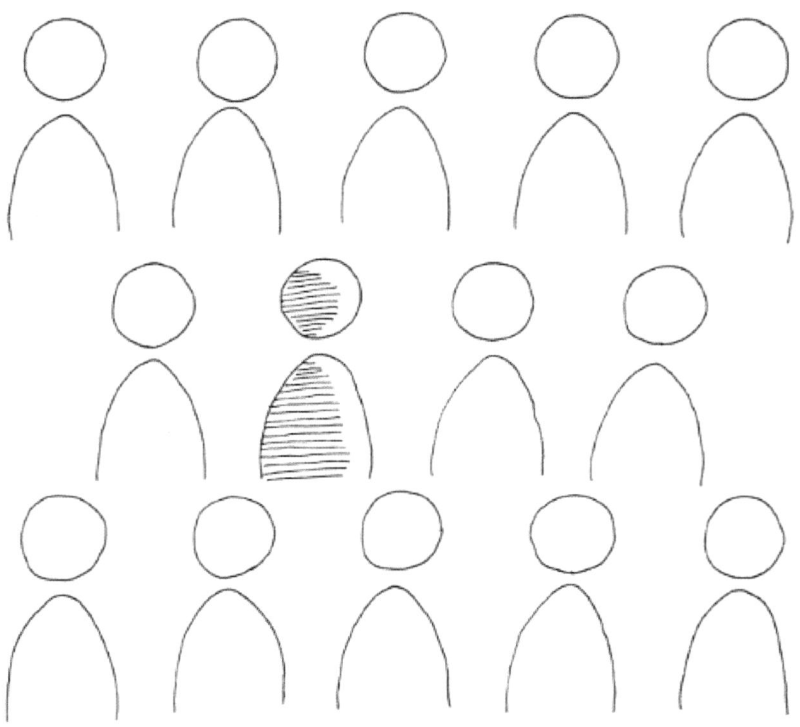

"Leader"

I remember following in their footsteps.
Eagerly proceeding in their pursuit of identity.
I looked to the masks that they wore
And felt humiliated
That I would never
Be like them.

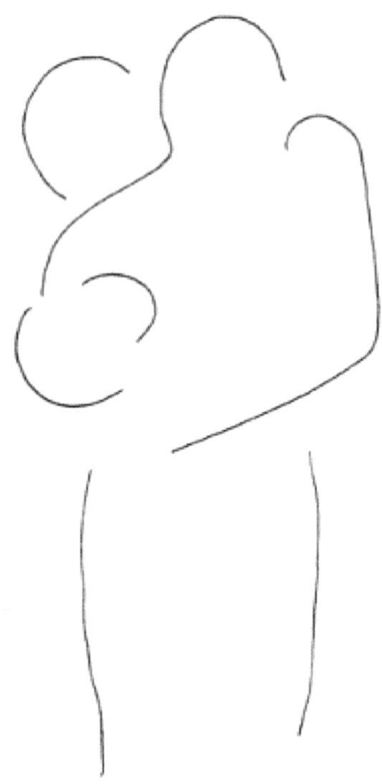

"Stitches"

I keep myself held together,
Not by thread
But by stitches.
There have been too many times
Where I have allowed my grip to be loosened
And opened to those who never reciprocated
The care to piece me back together
When I couldn't do it myself.

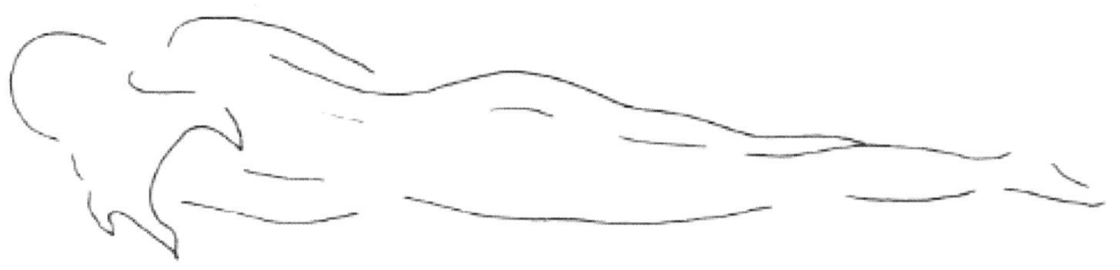

"Truth"

I shielded my eyes from what people had to say about you.
Withdrew the truth of the preconceived notion
That you loved me.
You gave me light,
You made me vivid.
I didn't want to let go of your beam,
But it turns out
That your sun glowed for another woman.

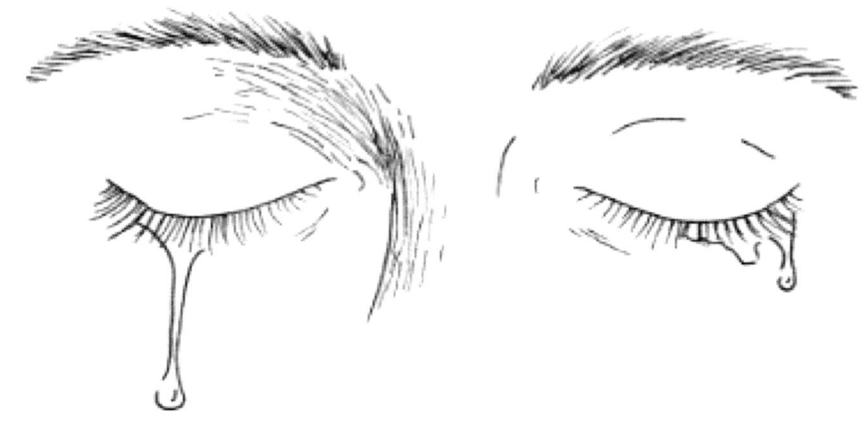

"The war waged in silence"

Without guns
Bullets
Bombs;
Deaths that passed in unacknowledged memoriam
Tears that did not water the bouquets.'
The war waged in silence
And ended
Without a single ally.

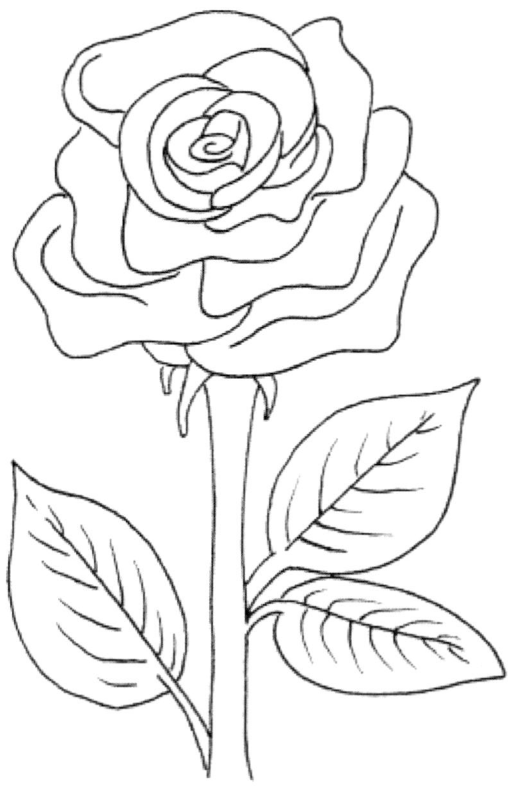

"Colour"

I wear colour to make myself feel less dull
And I'm starting to forget what being bright felt like.

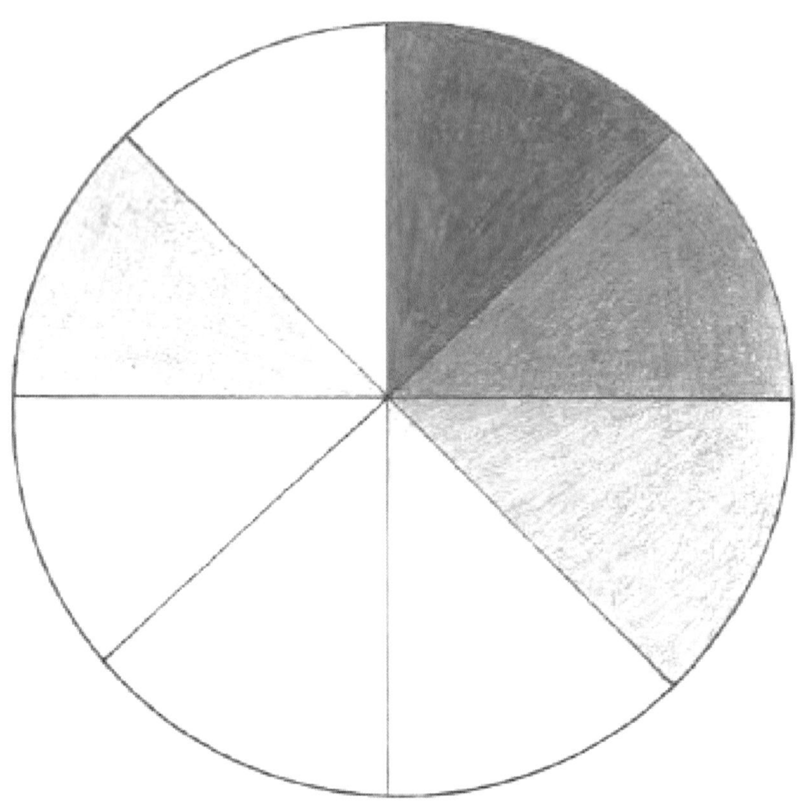

"Black and White"

I've seen so much black and white
That I forgot that there are colours
And people can show different ones too.

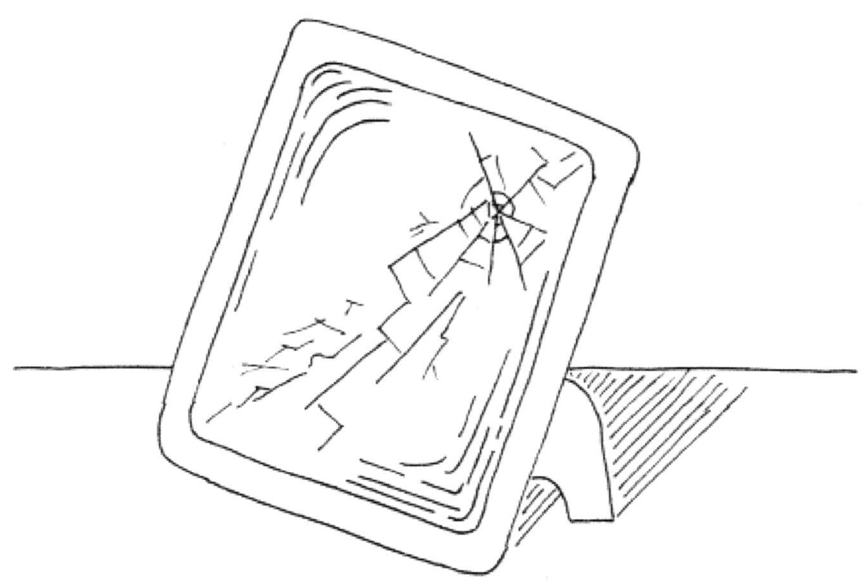

"Reflection"

I look to the mirror
And see my reflection.
A physical manifestation
That there are more days to come.
Even in the moments when there is a crack
In the image of hope,
I will be happy again.

Exoskeleton

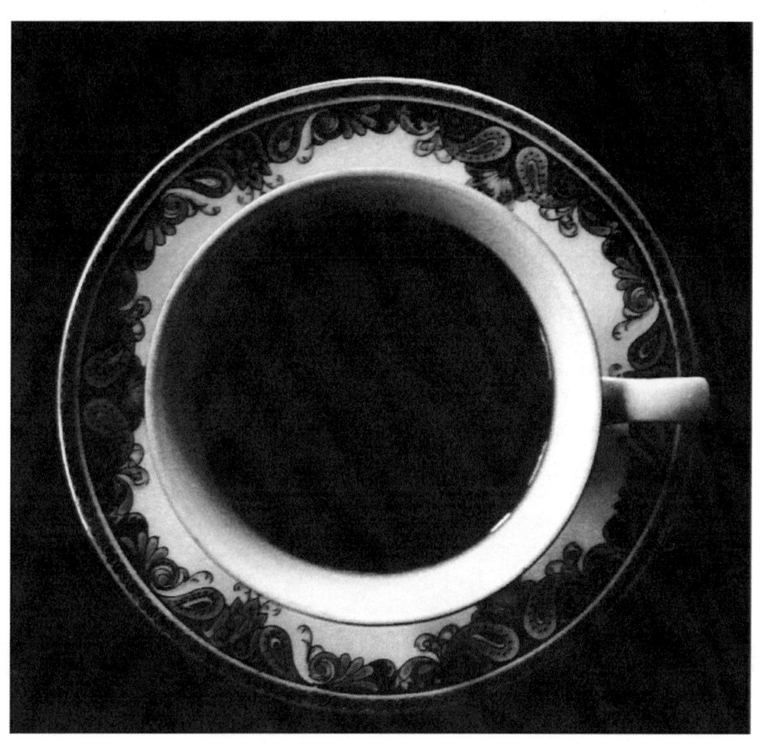

"Lukewarm"

I was raised to be warm.
To never settle the air with a cold draft
Or turn my shoulder with intent to numb.
The more heat I gave
The less heat I felt
And I became lukewarm.

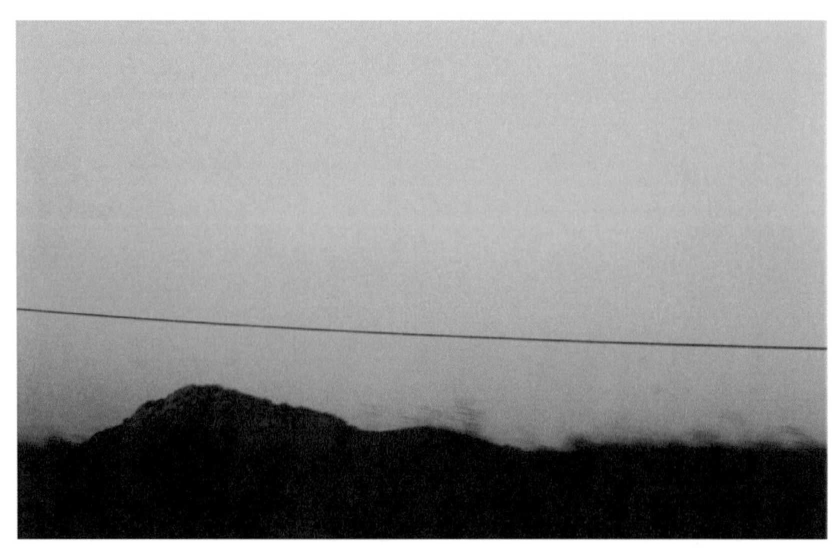

"Fill Hollow"

I tried to talk to someone.
Words never spill.
I just weep
Like an infant
Searching for the breast;
Waiting for the pain to be pacified.
I laid there
With my head against the couch
Tongue scared to meet speech
And verbalize the torment
That still haunts my soul.

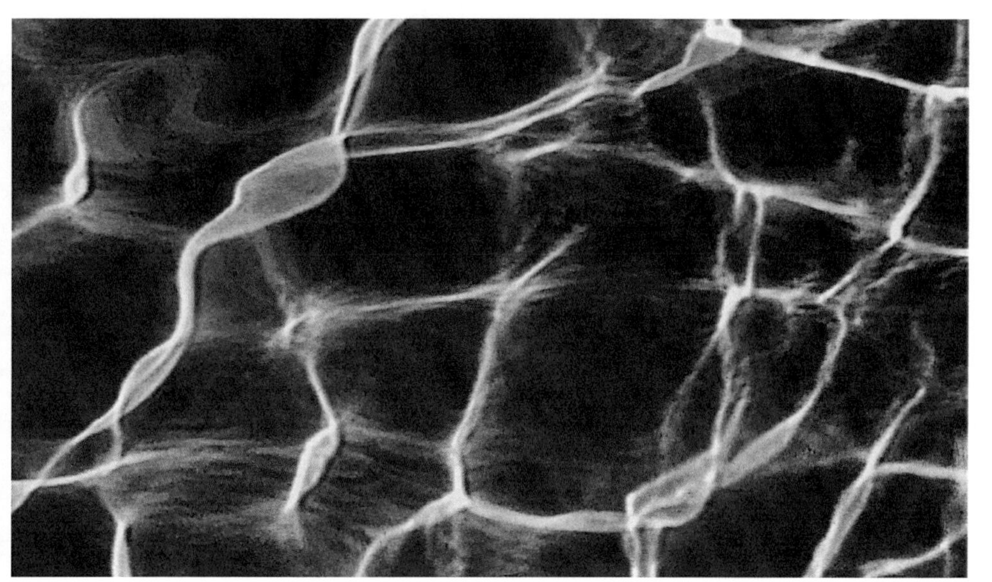

"Ode to Me"

You have always smiled.
You have always gone to those who never understood
What it was like to smile.
You have always gravitated towards those
Who never felt
The force of love.
You have always given a piece of yourself
To those who were ripped from wholeness.
Each part that you gave
Was a substitute for the gaps that needed filling.
You have done everything
For the sake of seeing light in someone else's eyes

That you forgot yours was dimming.
Yours was dimming because instead of light
You saw grey in the things that were happy
And you were left joyless.
And you were left
And you were left
And you were left.

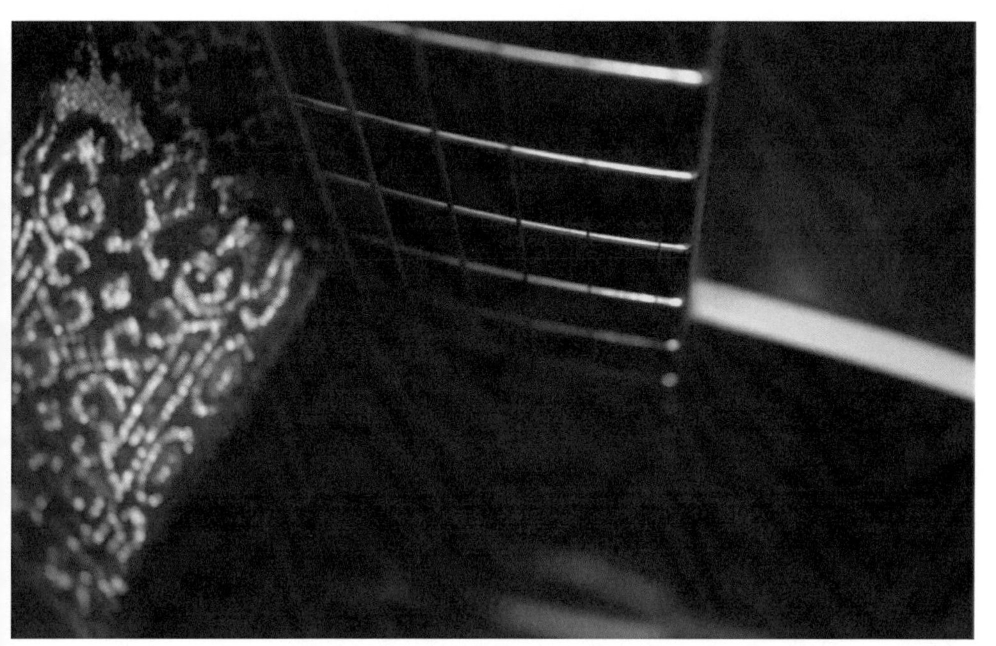

"Bitter"

Strings and caffeine
Plucked away the bitter taste
Of this depression.

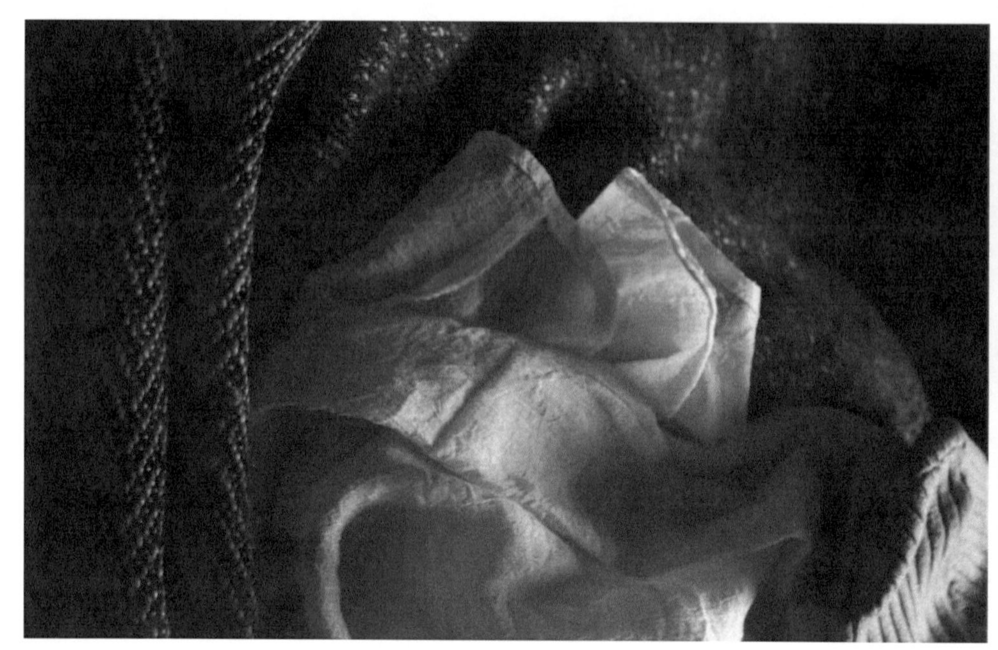

"Parts of you"

Were left to fill the gaps
Dug by those
Undeserving of your fullness.

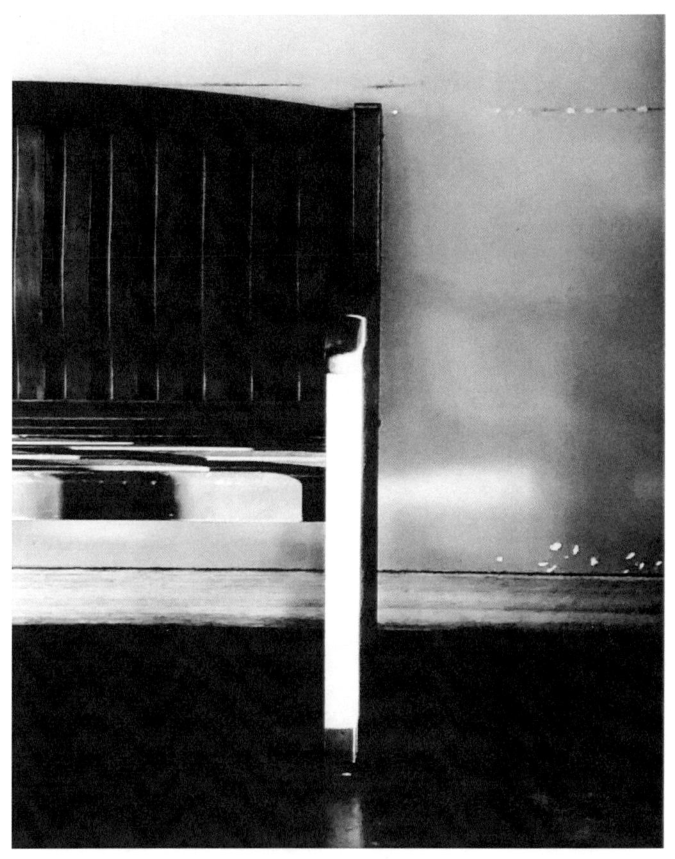

"Other"

I wish you were here on the porch with me. I wish to feel your hands on my hands, reassuring me that your love will help build this force of comfort around my heart. I want your voice to break through the yells and screams of the present and a past gluttonous in its attempts to fill my spirit with sorrow. I wish to see your eyes, eyes that look at me with love and only love. I wish you were here to heal me.

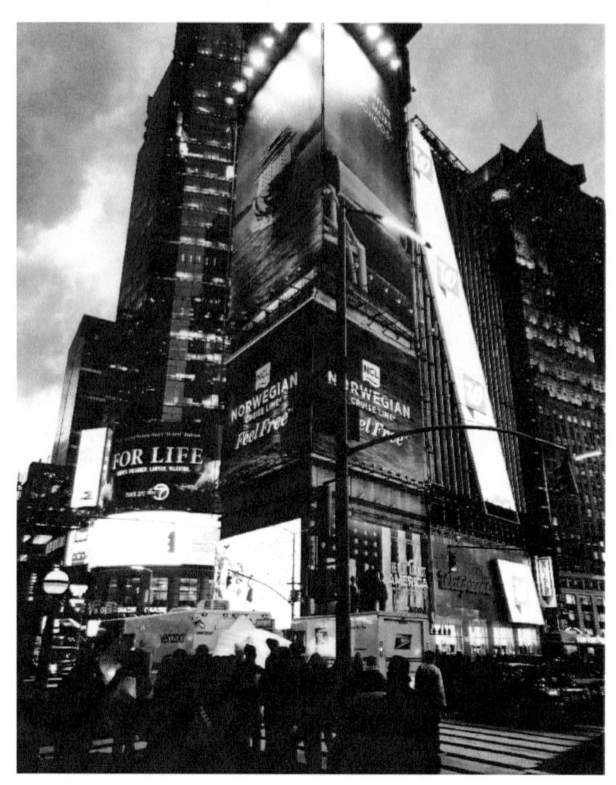# "Weight"

I didn't ask to be picked up
But you lifted the weight I felt
And gathered it in your hands.
A selfless gesture
That put a smile on my face
After days of pain
And I am grateful for your humility.

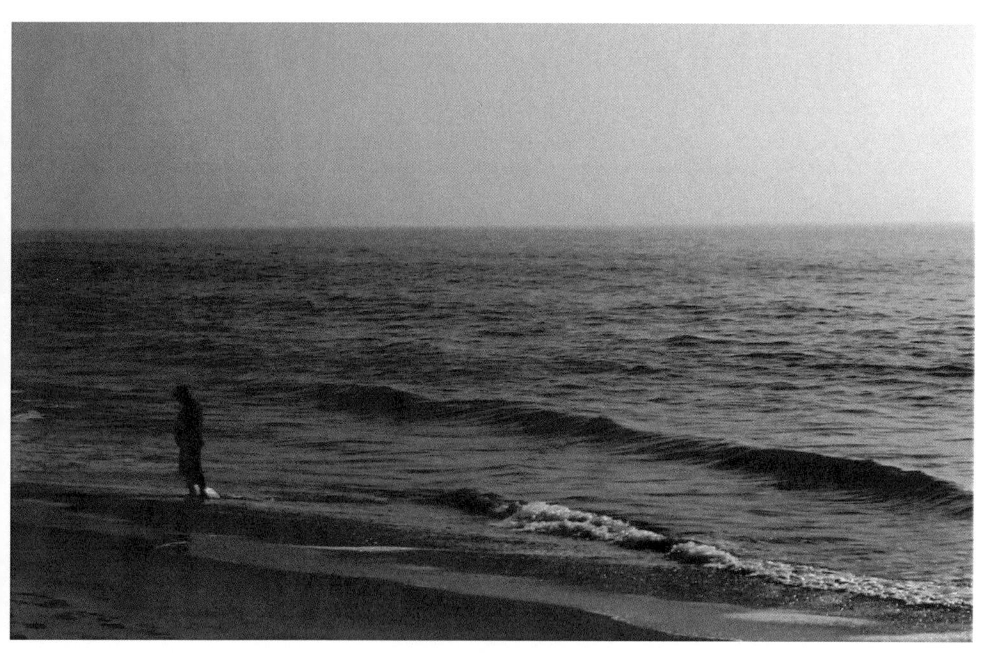

"Revision"

My skin is littered in stories.
Interpret them as you will.
Just promise that you will help me
Rewrite them.

Equilibrium

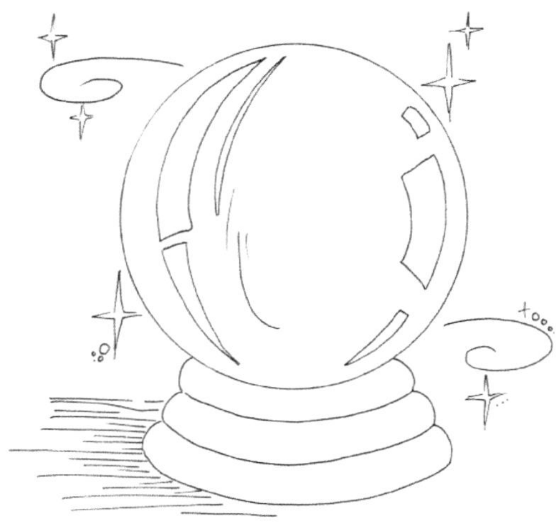

"Halves"

I can spend my well-earned money on rose quartz;
Meet the psychic down in Old Town
In a little shed to the left of First Street,
Have her read my palm or my cards,
Ask that she tunes in to whatever frequency God is in.
She will ask why
And I will keep my answer simple.
"I feel so close to him,
I can feel his skin on my fingertips
I can hear his voice beckon in the nights
and coo in the mornings.
If he is near,
Why have I been left in silence?"

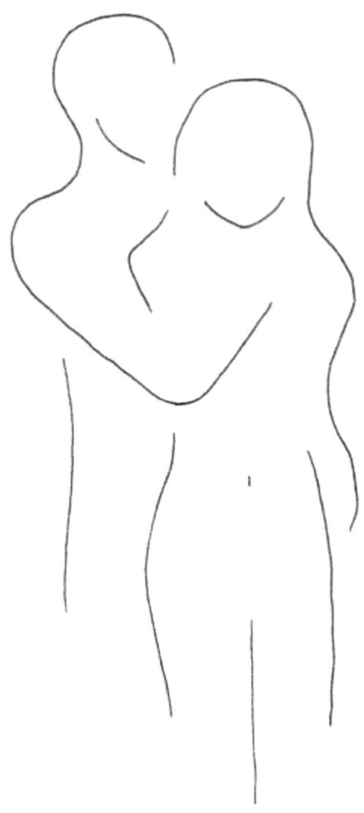

"Infinity Forever"

Play a tune,

And I will dance to chords meant for lovers.

I will move my body and become a rhythm

To the song that is graced with

Hands intertwining and bodies embracing each other in the hold
of love.

Their voices singing

Infinity forever.

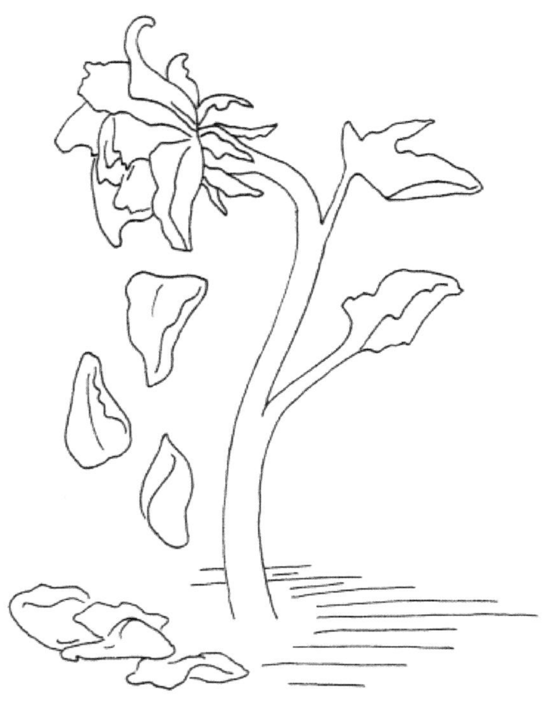

"Picking Petals"

I pick petals to lovers that are potential
And I am always left with a single bud
And not a full flower.
But you came and I bloomed
And it isn't even spring yet.

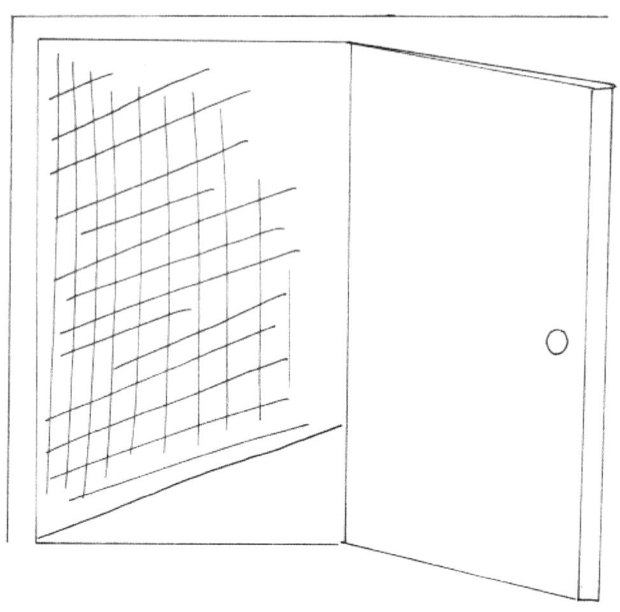

"Be Mine"

I want to open you up;
Reveal whatever enigmatic force
lives behind your eyes
So, I could name how you make me feel.
Do not hide from me, my love
I see the passion lurk
in the curve of your smirk
and in the question of your glance;
"Will you let me in?"

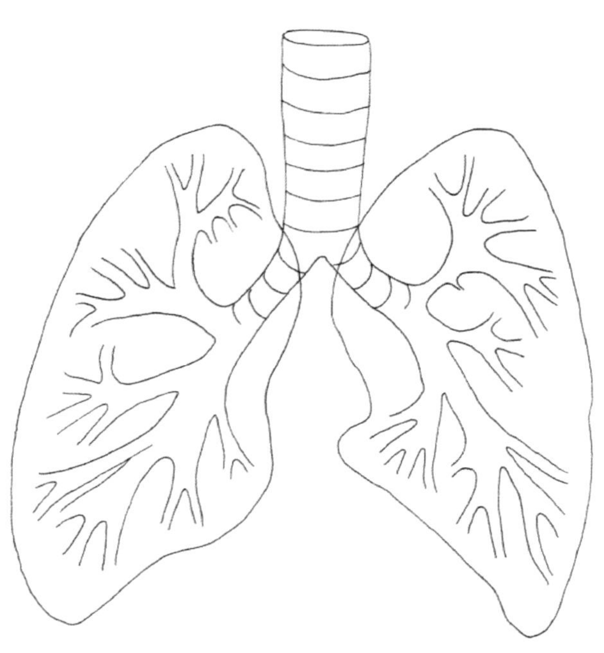

"Jealous"

I am jealous of your lungs
And how they breathe you in.
I am jealous of your lips
And of your tongue;
Greedy that they always taste a potential kiss
And I am jealous of your hands
And how they touch your skin.
I want to crawl within you
And experience each of these things.

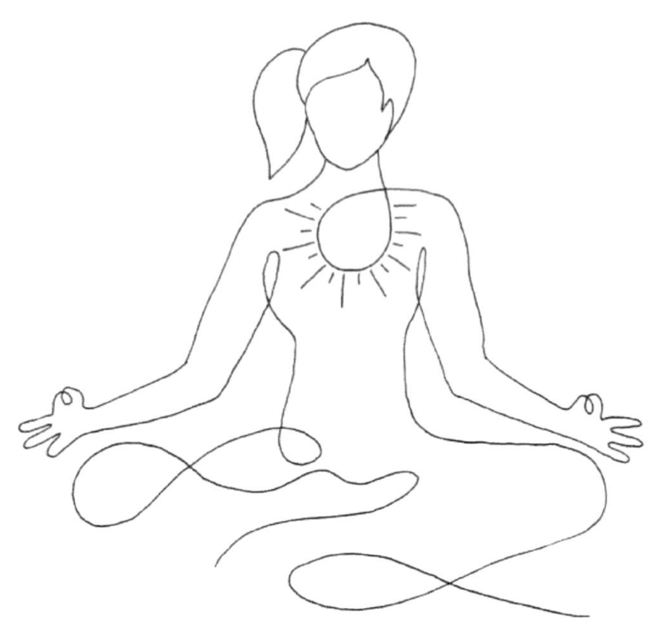

"Miracle"

It was the summer of 2018.
I felt a change in the season.
An emotional
And spiritual shift.
My intuition gave sight
Towards the blur of what was to come.
The smoke cleared
And you submerged from the haze-
My miracle.

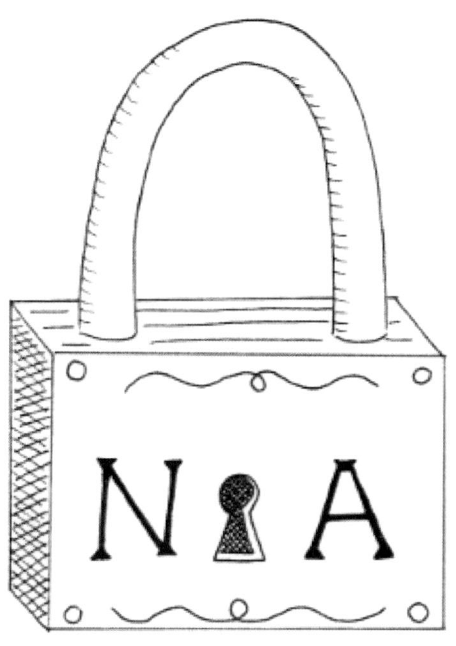

"Lock"

There are sublevels to my person.

Each designed to either protect or hide.

You passed each barrier and each lock without a key.

And in that,

I knew to keep you.

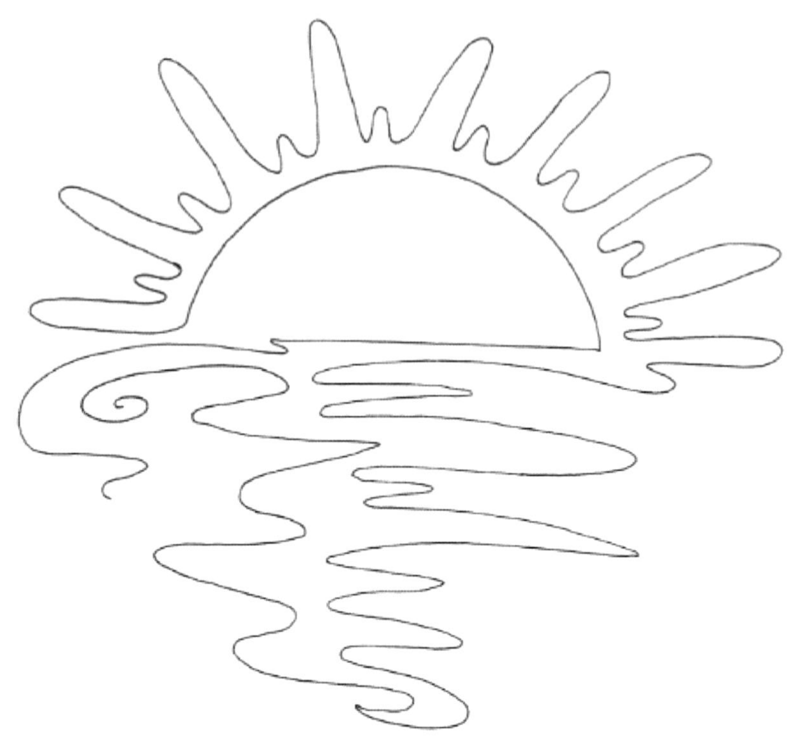

"Child of the Sun"

You burned in me.
I basked in your rays
And became light.

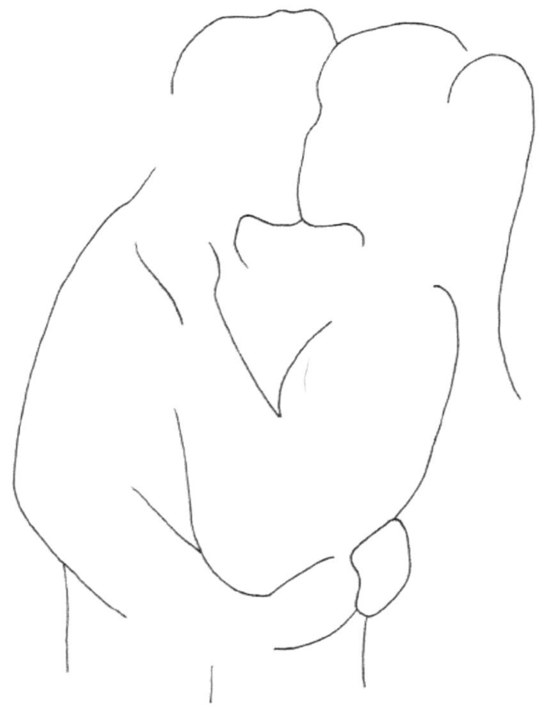

"Furiously"

Love me furiously.
The red-hot flush of your love
Taints my body and I am glowing in your blush.
Let me shine
And be your sun.

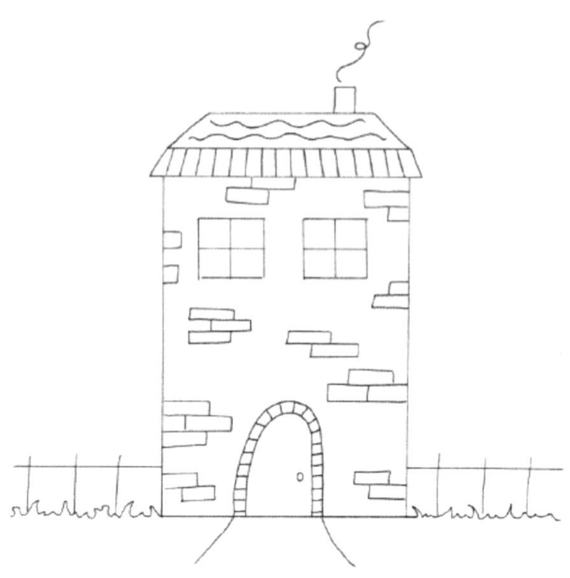

"Gentle"

The morning has just arisen.
Do not disturb its awakening.
Play the music softly,
Stir the coffee slowly,
Kiss your lover gently.
Wear your lightest robe,
Pick up your feet when you walk,
Glide through your home.
Mimic the Divine.
Do not speak over this peace.

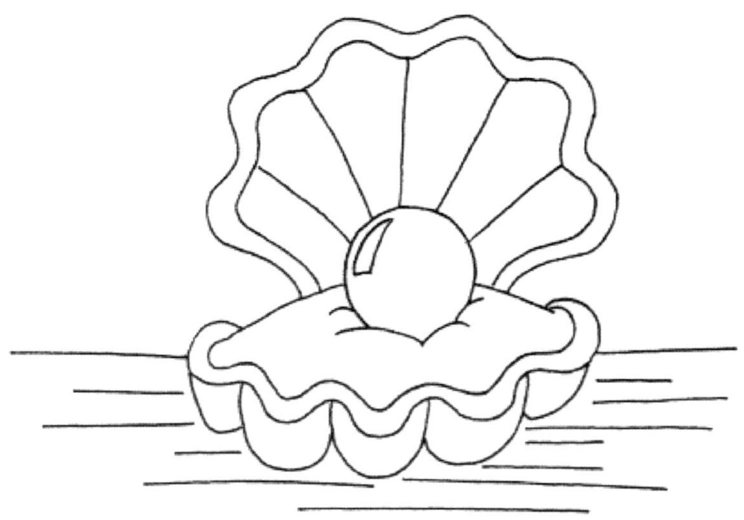

"Gem"

You were the hidden gem
Not to be given
But to be received.
I finally have you.

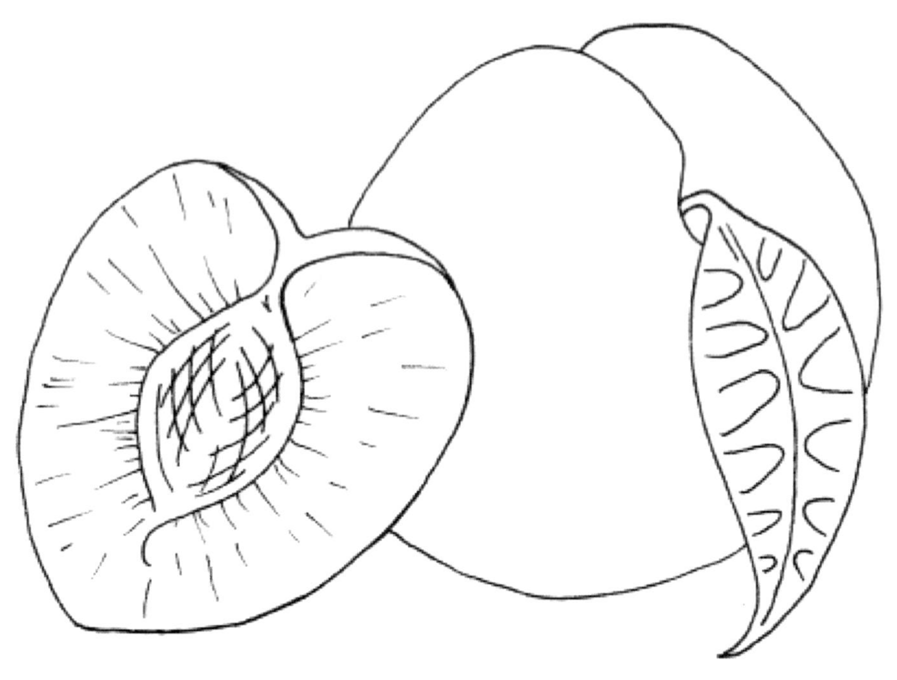

"Fruit"

If you tempt me
With the fruits of your skin,
I may or may not take a bite
And leave you seedless.

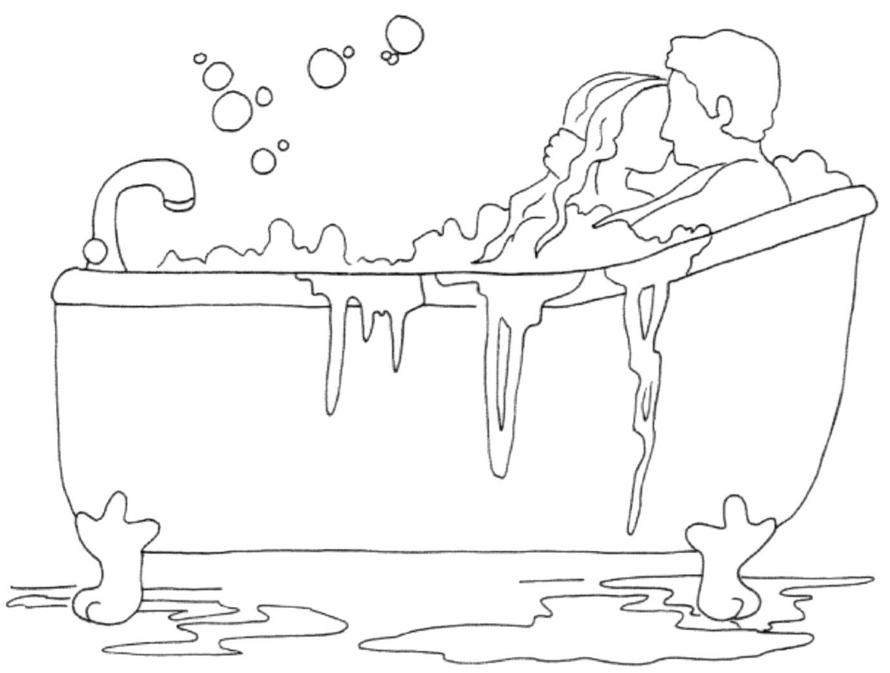

"Bask"

For the first time,

I let the wind kiss my skin

And I settled where you were.

The sun set and you became the horizon.

Shedding your night

I dimmed in your glow.

A balance of light and dark

That made The Perfect Warmth.

Those beside me shuffled in your brilliance,

But I stayed to bask in you.

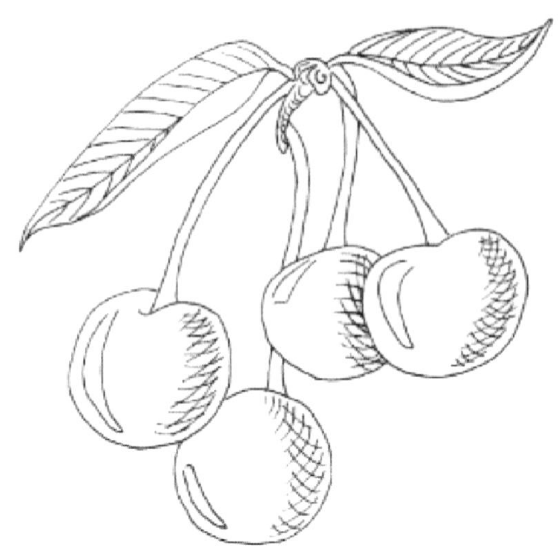

"Honey"

The first sunny day in two weeks.
Conversations spent under the sun,
Warmth kissing the skin
Of bodies sitting on the grass,
Talking amongst the leaves.
A moment of silence passed
As the wind changed
And brought the breeze of you.
Hair like honey
Golden and thick
With red lips
Like cherries inside of my mouth,
Staining my tongue with the taste of you.

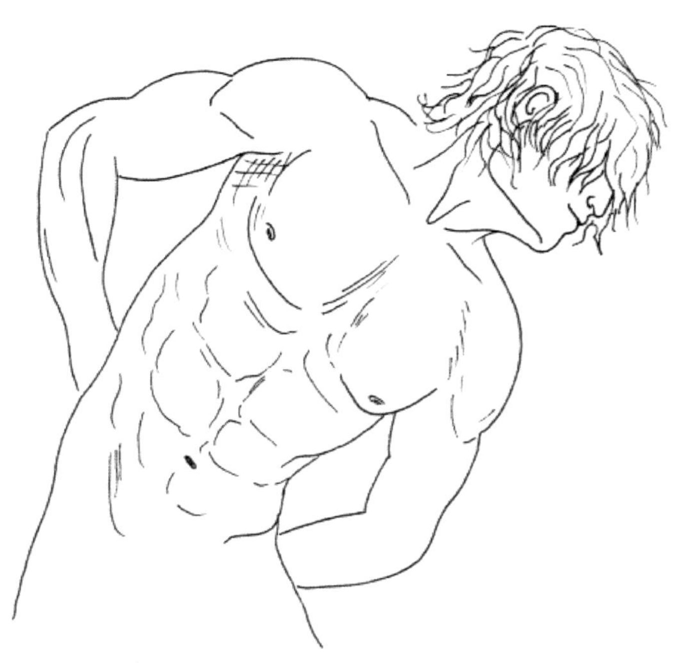

"Conclude this rendezvous"

Fear not of my mortality.
Spend your infinity
In my limits.
Look to conclude this rendezvous
With a kiss.
I will die happily for the last time;
You,
For the first.

"Jade"

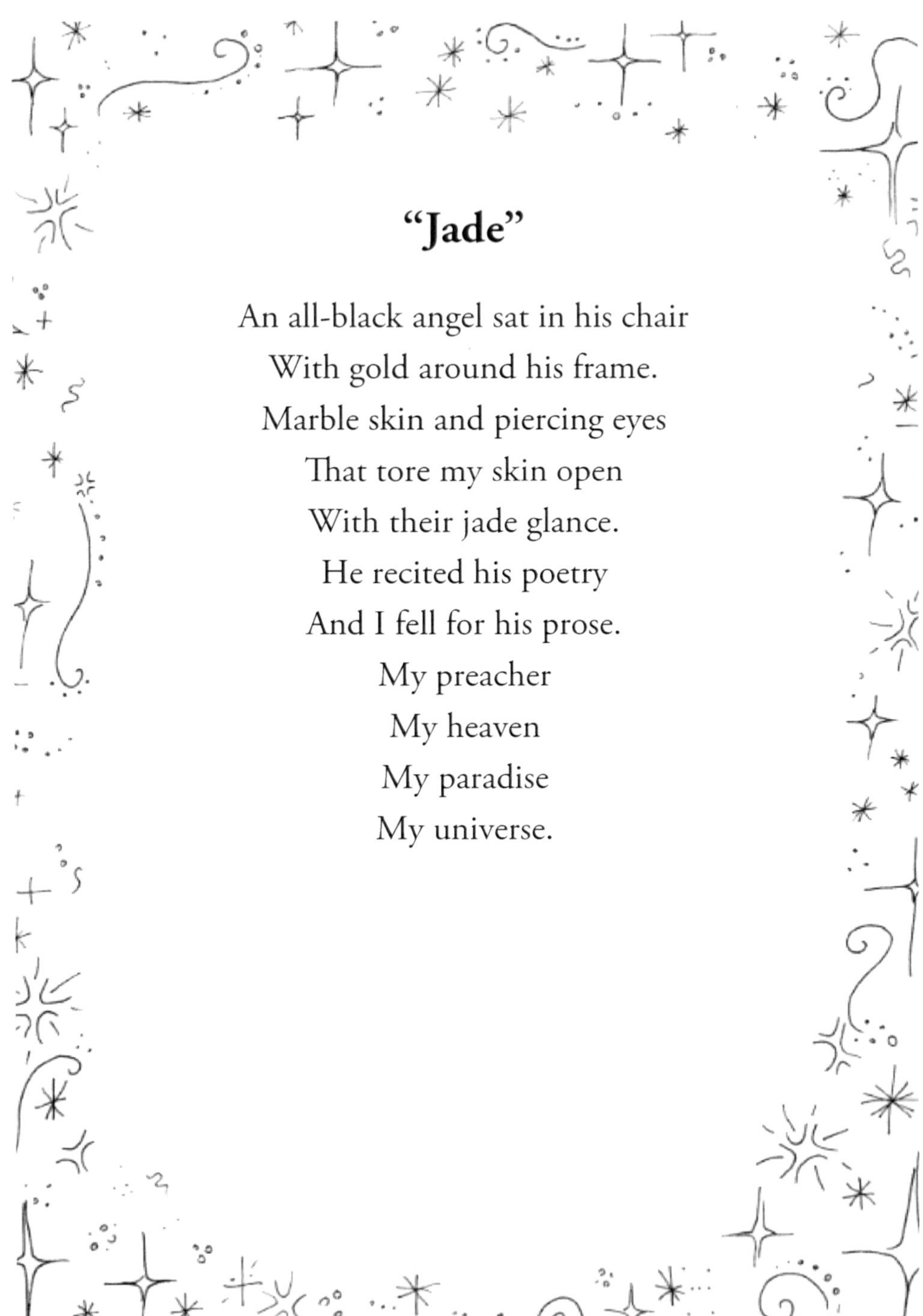

An all-black angel sat in his chair
With gold around his frame.
Marble skin and piercing eyes
That tore my skin open
With their jade glance.
He recited his poetry
And I fell for his prose.
My preacher
My heaven
My paradise
My universe.

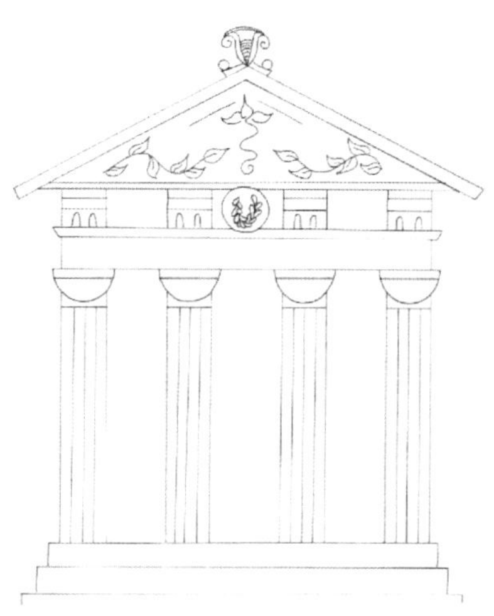

"Heaven"

Heaven is not a figment of fabrication.

Heaven has a physical form and he is Lying beside me.

I called for him and God

Gifted me the blessing of his kiss.

The touch of his lips on mine rattled the Earth

The same way Adam first touched Eve.

Skin soft and silky

He fell into her body's temptation.

One taste and he sang with his hands in her hair.

Heaven is not just a dream or a state of mind.

Heaven has arms,

And he is waiting for me to come home.

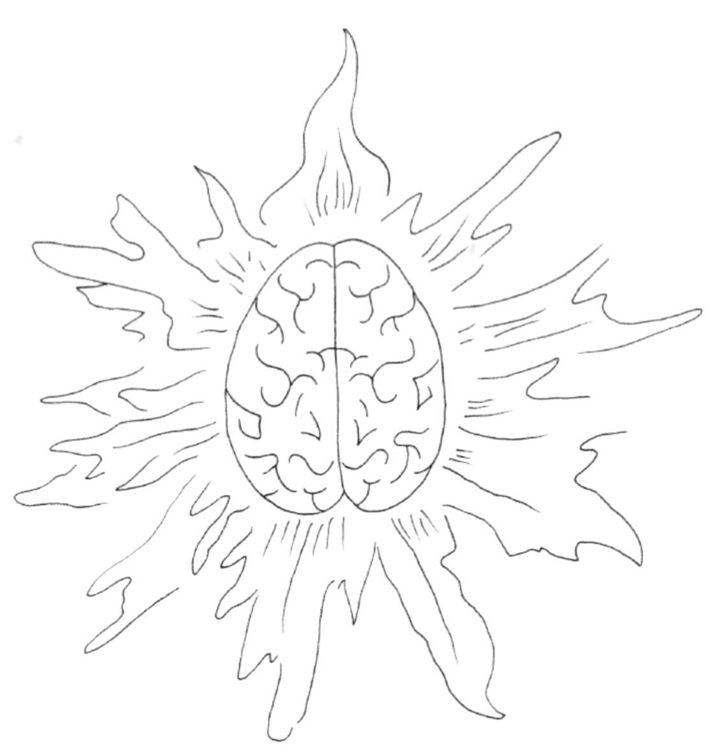

"Impulse"

Forgive me if I act on impulse,
I think of you
And you become my sudden urge.

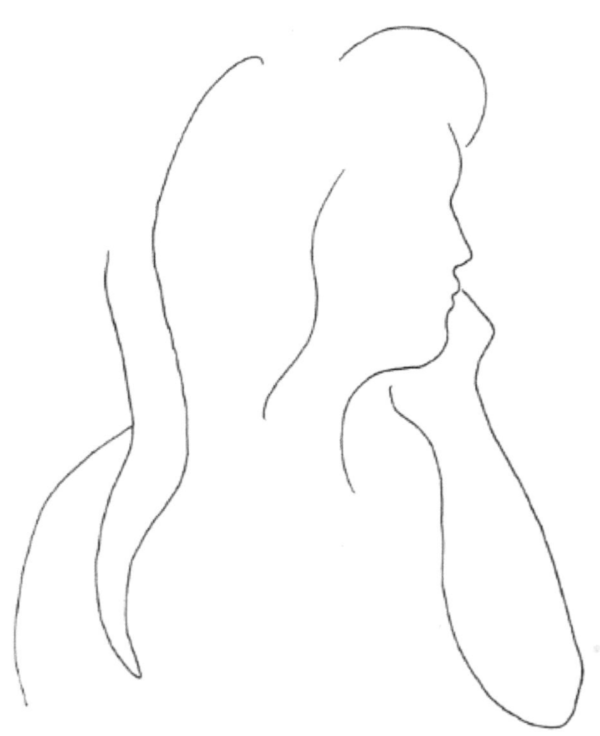

"Idle"

Any moment longer in idle
You consume the space in between.
I love having you infiltrate my mind.

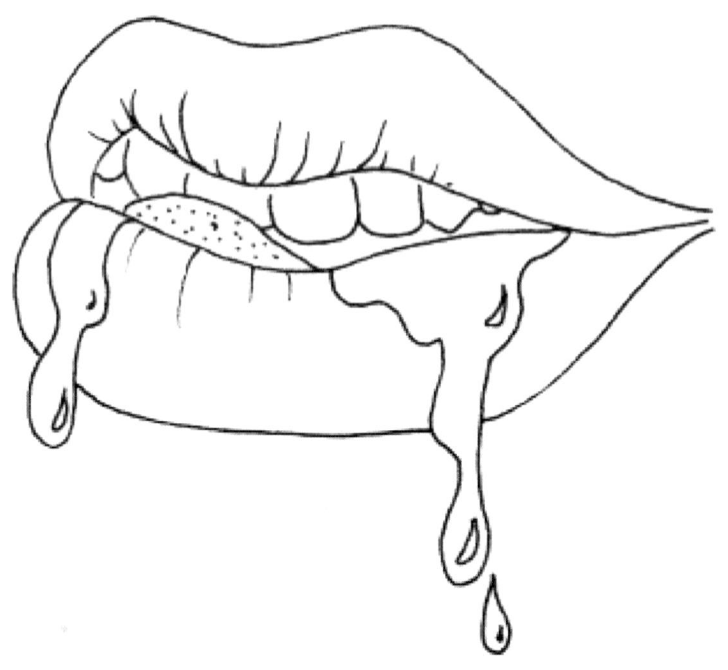

"Taste"

I hope that when we kiss
You can taste what I feel for you.

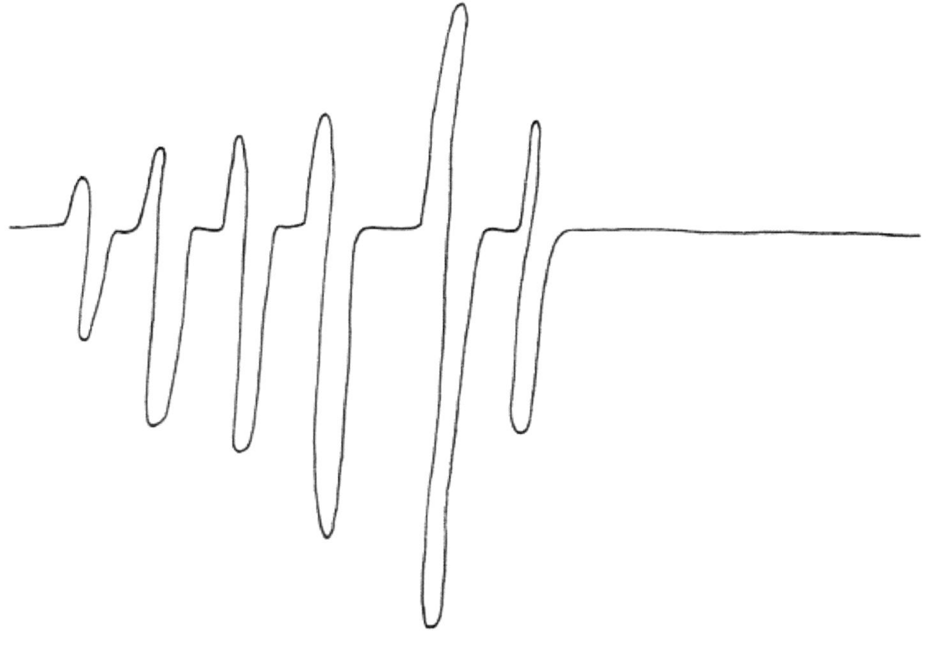

"Pause in you"

Quiet down
The movement ceases
And I pause in your presence.

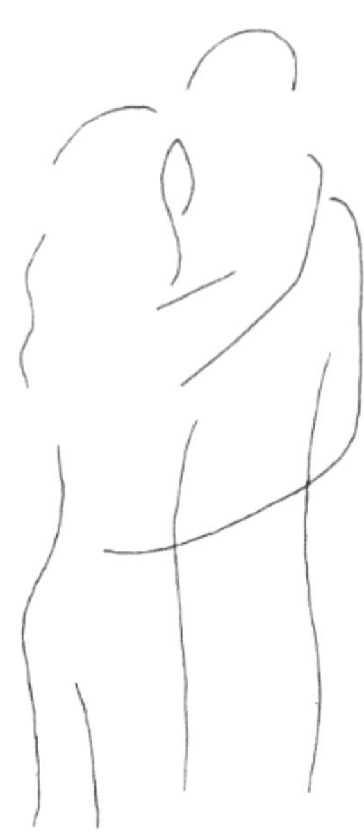

"Heat"

Your head is against my chest.
Curls tangled
And your cheek rests on my skin.
Hands on both sides of my frame
Lightly caressing the skin
That is now yours.
I look down
And see your body atop mine.
All I feel is your heat.

The Unrequited

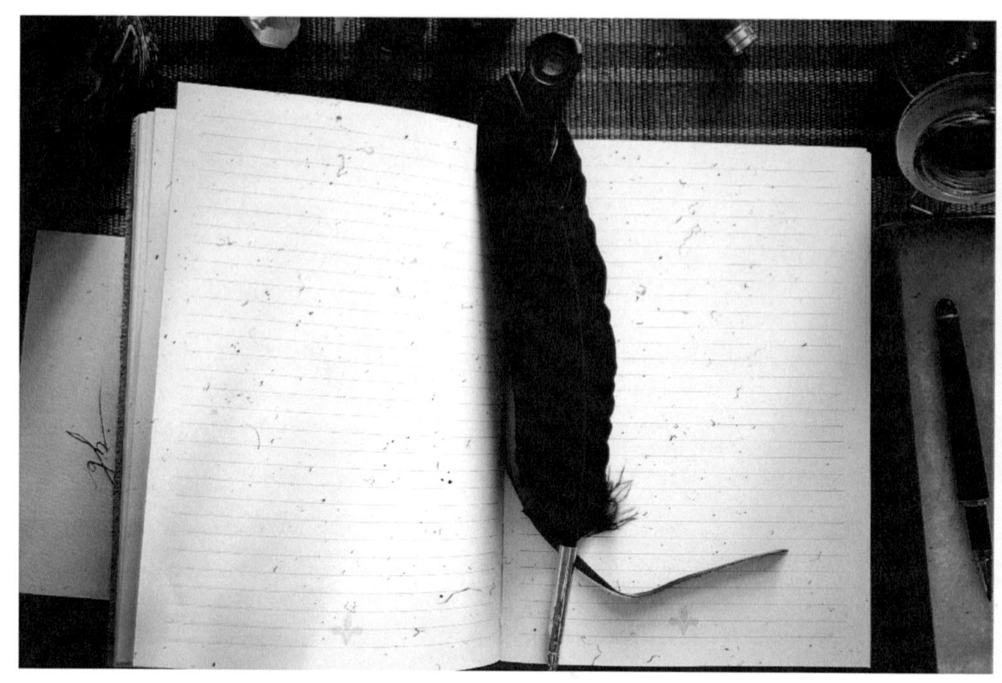

"For you"

I wrote to you,

About you,

For you,

And against you.

These feelings have been expressed

To the dead air that surrounds us.

You will never hear these words

From my lips

But as you read this,

You will understand my silence.

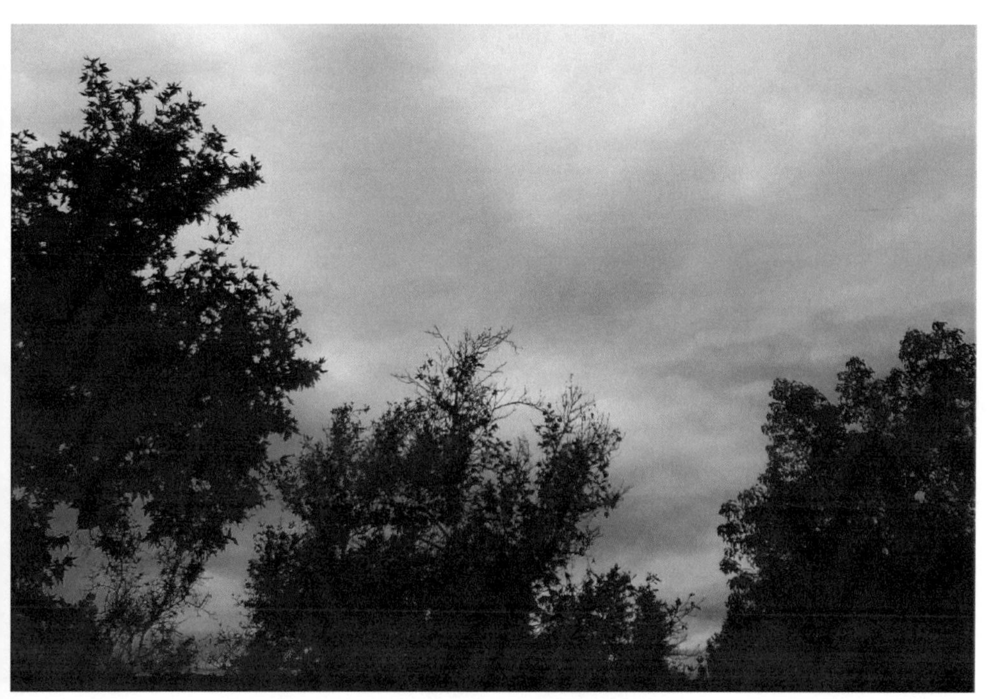

"Seasons"

We were heat in the summer
But December came
And winter passed with our feelings
And promises.

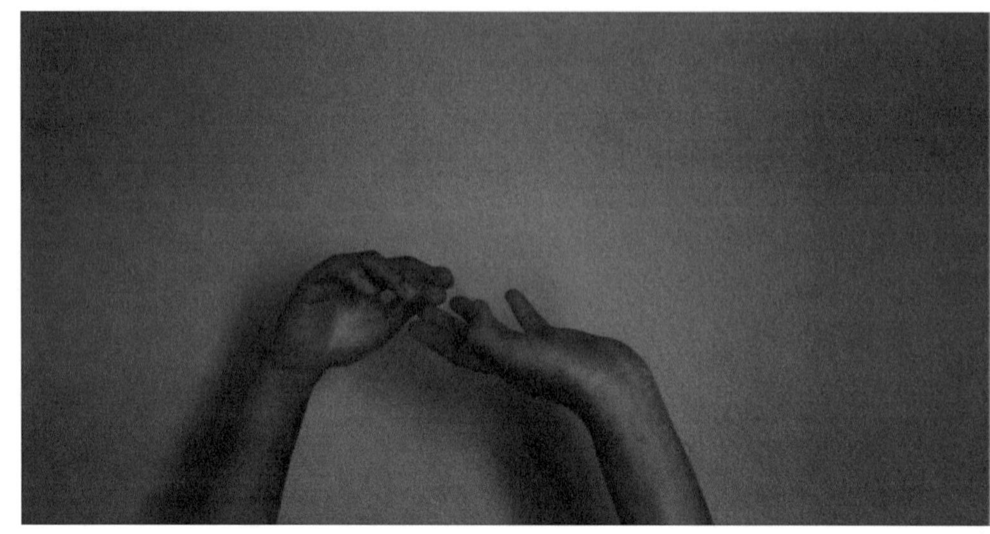

"Freedom"

She is freedom

And he loves his liberation

After being enslaved by my grip.

I held him as long as I could

Because his hands were the only hands I ever held.

His fingers were slipping

But I persisted to keep them interlocked with mine

And she was pulling him

But I could not keep him from leaving.

So, I watched

as he became hers to touch.

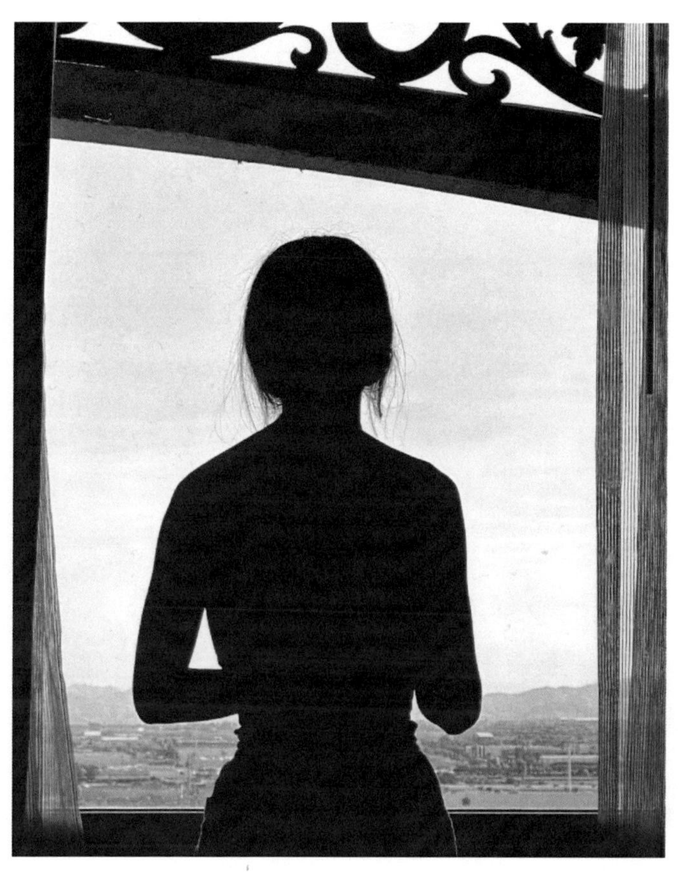

"Walls"

You kept me away in the farthest corners of your mind
While you went to her,
With her walls surrounding you.

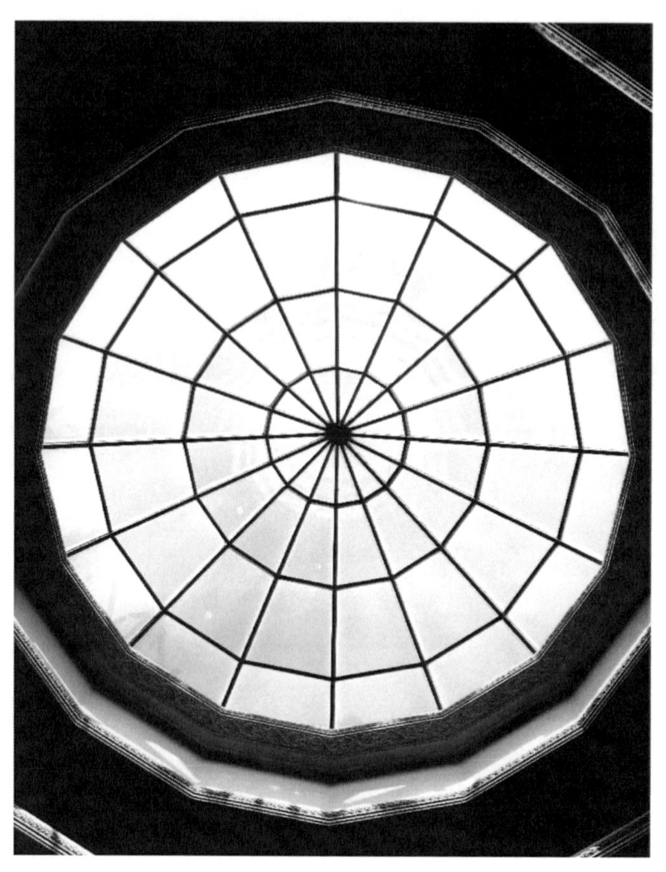

"Cycle"

These conversations are no longer genuine.
Just recurring attempts to expel the silence
And bring light
To illusive sound.

"Flee"

I no longer chase the thought of us;
It was always fleeting
And I learned
To never try
And catch fate.

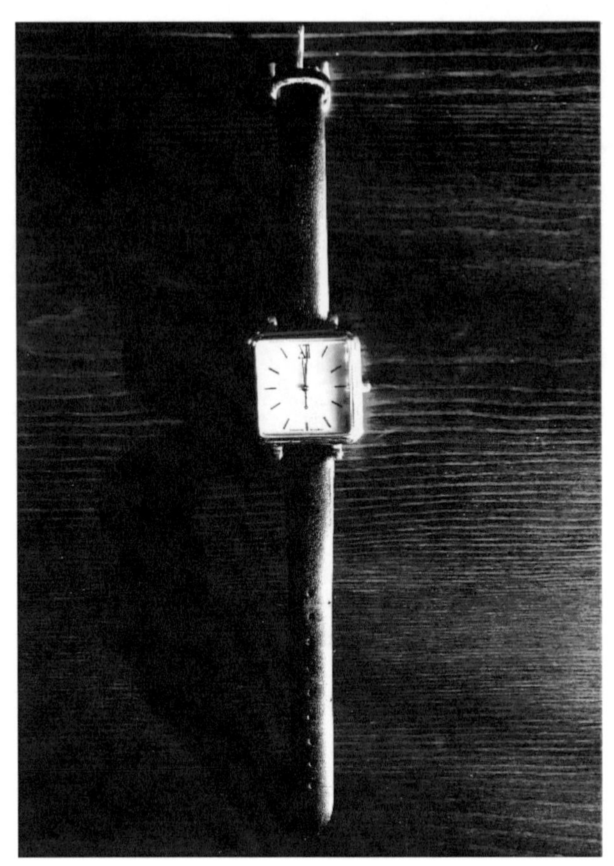

"Chime"

Each tick is a thought
And each tock is a tease
To indecision.
Rotational doubt
Circumference's hope.
"What if?"

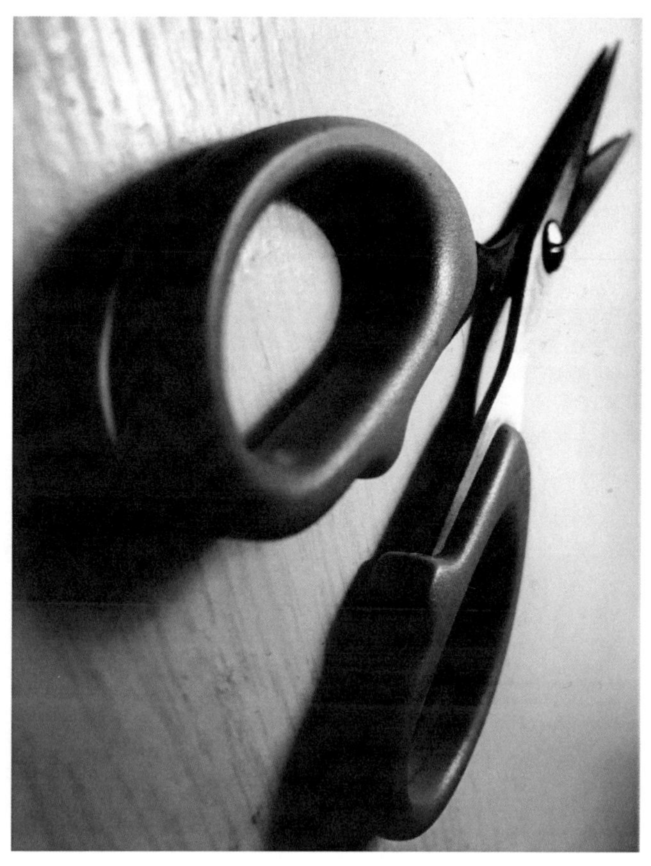

"Guillotine"

Cut my tongue.
Sever the idea that I would change your mind.
There is no mending to words
That have already been torn.

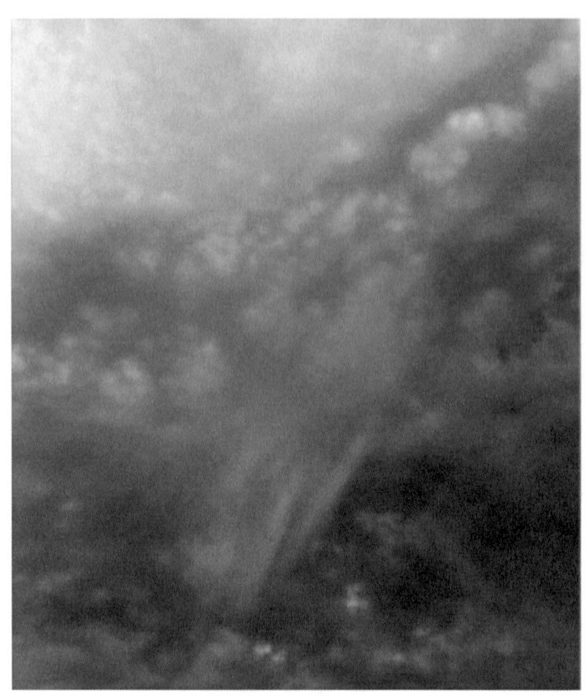

"Misplaced Cherubs"

Your rightful place is in the kingdom.
Each one of them shook their heads
With calm eyes
And a kind smile,
"We came here
To mend the broken ones."

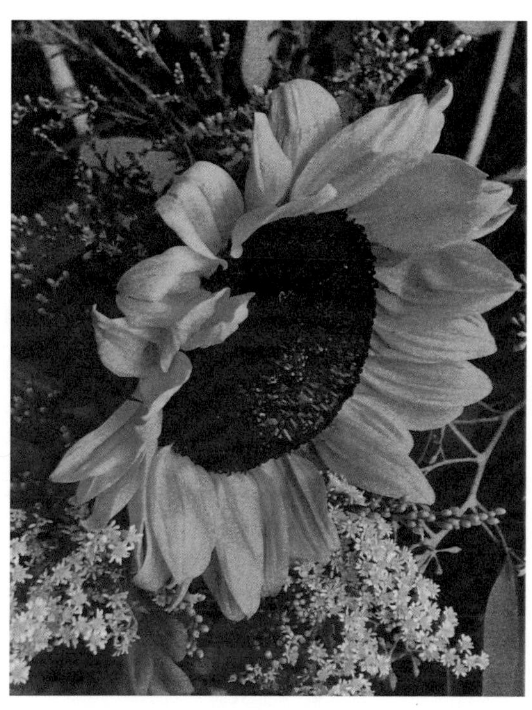

"Flora"

The flowers around me don't wilt;
Rather they turn their petals towards
The rims of their vases
And bend their stems to fit back into their fetal bloom.
Nature knows when to silence herself
And how to begin anew.
It would be good for us humans
To turn our petals inward from time to time.

The Mending

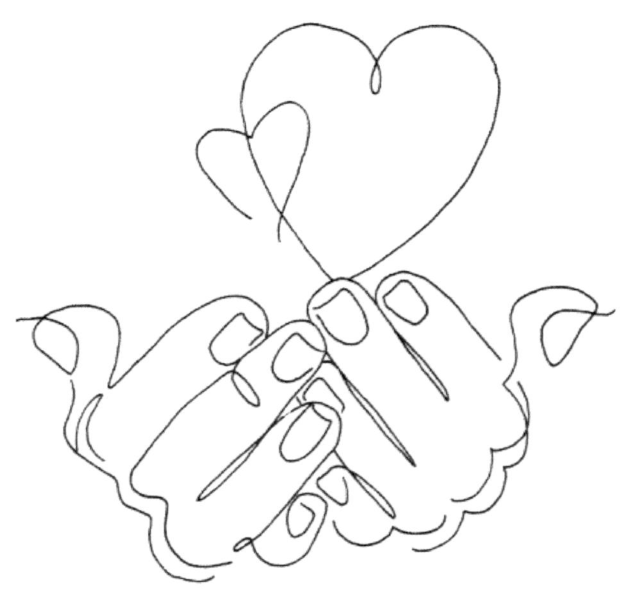

"Burrowing"

Burrow,

In dirt that is properly soiled.

Cocoon,

Upon a branch that is sturdy.

Swim,

In water that is calm.

Go,

Where you will be loved

Unconditionally.

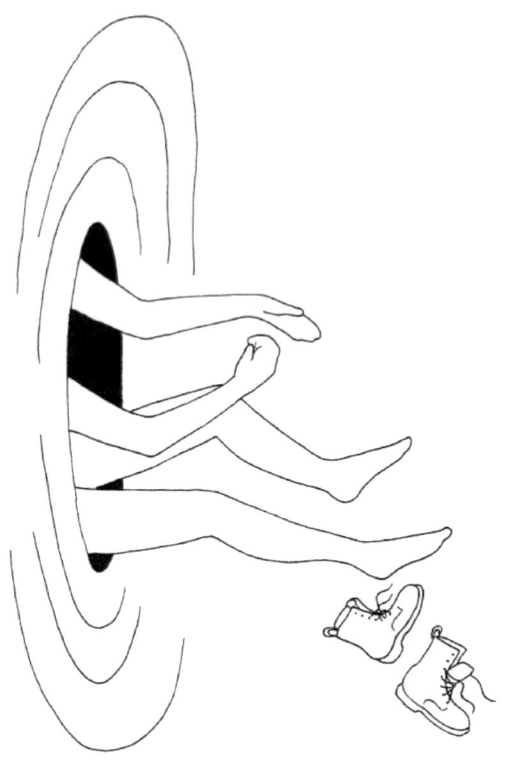

"Bottom"

Never settle for less. No matter how good they tell you
things are going to be, you will be left at the bottom with their
love out of reach.

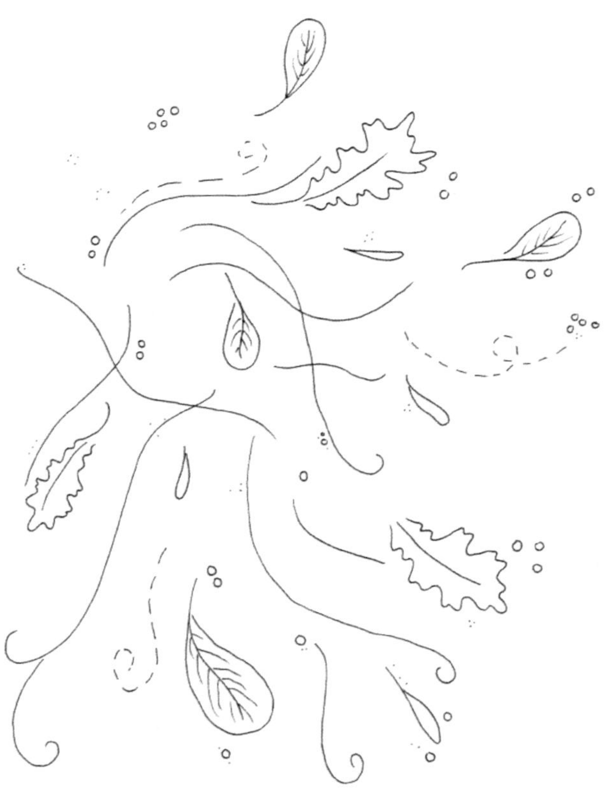

"Last Season"

May the last bits of this season
Carry the pieces of you
as a whole
To the next.

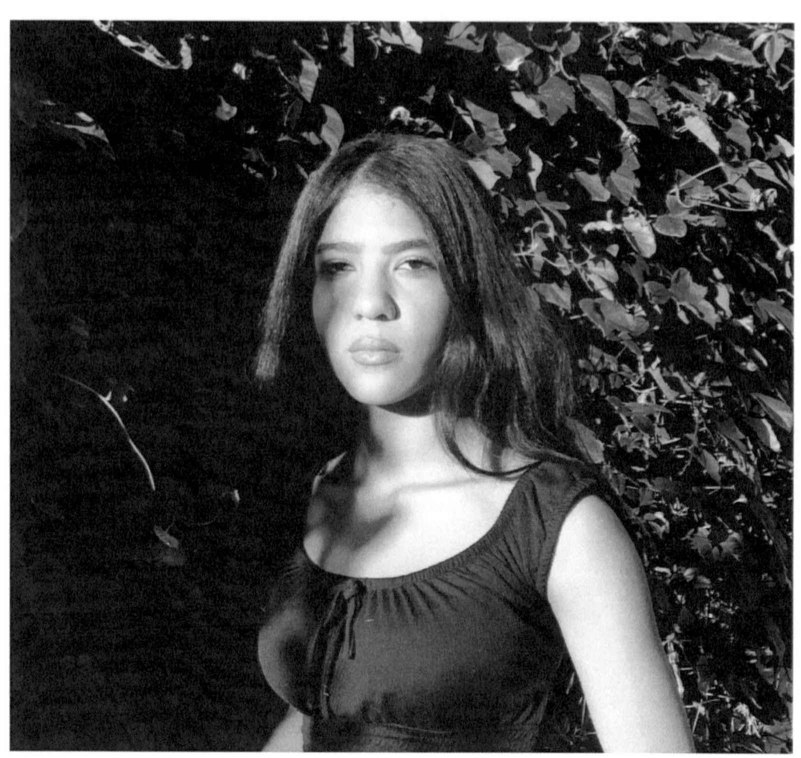

About the Author

G.K. is an eighteen-year-old singer-songwriter and poet. Born and raised in the sunny hills of California, she tends to find herself drinking far too much tea and writing until the most unreasonable hours of the night. She currently resides with her mother and father, older brother and sister and their husky. When she is not writing, she enjoys the company of both her friends and family, and simply just living in the present moment. If you would like to see more of her, you can follow her on Instagram at gabrielawarrenmusic and listen to her original music on every free-streaming music platform.